Anger Management

Simple Hacks to Control Your Anger and Manage Your Temper. Improve Your Overall Mood, Relationships and Quality of Life!

Robert S. Lee

© Copyright 2019 by Robert S. Lee- All rights reserved.

This document is geared toward providing exact and reliable information in regard to the topic and issue covered. The publication is sold with the idea that the publisher is not required to render accounting, officially permitted, or otherwise, qualified services. If advice is necessary, legal or professional, a practiced individual in the profession should be ordered.

- From a Declaration of Principles which was accepted and approved equally by a Committee of the American Bar Association and a Committee of Publishers and Associations.

In no way is it legal to reproduce, duplicate, or transmit any part of this document in either electronic means or in printed format. Recording of this publication is strictly prohibited and any storage of this document is not allowed unless with written permission from the publisher. All rights reserved.

The information provided herein is stated to be truthful and consistent, in that any liability, in terms of inattention or otherwise, by any usage or abuse of any policies, processes, or directions contained within is the solitary and utter responsibility of the recipient reader. Under no circumstances will any legal responsibility or blame be held against the publisher for any reparation, damages, or monetary loss due to the information herein, either directly or indirectly.

Respective authors own all copyrights not held by the publisher.

The information herein is offered for informational purposes solely, and is universal as so. The presentation of the information is without contract or any type of guarantee assurance.

The trademarks that are used are without any consent, and the publication of the trademark is without permission or backing by the trademark owner. All trademarks and brands within this book are for clarifying purposes only and are the owned by the owners themselves, not affiliated with this document.

Contents

Take a Deep Breath 1

Chapter 1. Identify the Cause of Your Anger ... 11

Chapter 2. Learn How to Express Yourself 20

Chapter 3. Learn Not to Express Yourself 29

Chapter 4. Set Some Healthy Boundaries 39

Chapter 5. Give Your Partner Equal Respect . 48

Chapter 6. Develop Hobbies As a Couple 57

Chapter 7. Develop Hobbies on Your Own 66

Chapter 8. Consider Couples Counseling 75

The Worst-Case Scenario 84

Take a Deep Breath

...and count to ten, because you're about to learn some things about yourself that you may not want to hear.

You have anger issues. You sometimes become infuriated without warning. Other times, you fail to express your anger when you should. It drives people away. It affects your own self-image, sometimes more than you realize. It even brings out the anger in others, to the extent that personalities may clash when you could have gotten along just fine.

Don't believe what you just read? That's fine...no one really expected you to. Unfortunately, that's part of the human condition. Nothing in the above paragraph was unique to you. Everyone has struggles with anger management from time to time, and most of them never realize it because they are so accustomed to thinking that they are normal. And they are, but "normal" isn't the same thing as "perfect" by a long shot.

It can be easy to fall into the trap of thinking that people only have anger issues when there is something fundamentally wrong with them, but the hard truth is that it doesn't take a chemical imbalance to send someone flying off the handle every once in a while. In fact, issues with anger management might even have a worse impact on those who do not struggle with it on a daily basis, as they are more likely to alter people's perceptions of them due to what appears to be an unexplained rash of mood swings.

If you have ever been in such a position, then you have likely learned that the effects of irrational displays of anger can have profound effects on one's personal relationships. This is especially true of romantic relationships, which must be built upon a sense of mutual trust that becomes difficult to maintain when one partner has succumbed to sudden displays of rage. Even expressions of annoyance or irritation that seem to take on a level of intensity unsuited for the situation may cause one's romantic partner to question whether or not you are the person that they thought you were.

Assuming that you care about your personal relationships—and one would certainly hope that this is a fair assumption—you are going to want to find a way to keep your anger in check. Of course, first you have to admit to yourself that you struggle with anger to begin with. If you really put your mind to it, you can probably think of some times when you were too controlling and prone to throw a temper tantrum when you didn't get your way. You can probably think of some times when you tried to be generous toward others, yet felt as if they owed you rather than simply doing a good deed for the sake of caring.

If you can think of some moments like those above, then you have already begun to see some of the more cunning ways in which anger can grip you without you even noticing. The good news is that once you have begun to see this, you can begin to do something about it.

The following chapters will walk you through some of the basic steps of managing anger in your relationships. Some of these steps may sound like general relationship advice, but in this case they will be tailored specifically to the effects that every positive action enumerated within this book can have on your mood.

These chapters have been arranged so that you may gradually grow accustomed to each of the following steps and allow yourself to grow as a person while minimizing the control that anger has on your personal relationships. Bear in mind that anger does not just manifest itself in the form of screaming and domestic violence, but even in the little twinges of annoyance you may experience that cause you to feel as if everything your partner says is grating.

The first chapter will focus on the need to identify the causes of your anger. This is easier said than done, but it is also simply than some might expect it to be.

The second and third chapters will cover the times when you should express yourself, as well as the times when you shouldn't. This will help you learn how to address the sources of your anger in a healthy fashion.

The fourth chapter will speak on the need to set boundaries for yourself in order to ensure that you will have less cause to succumb to anger in the future. The fifth chapter will cover the need to allow your partner to create boundaries as well, so as to prevent him or her from becoming angry and sparking a battle of emotions between the two of you.

Assuming that this does not completely solve the problem, the sixth and seventh chapters will cover how to find ways of appreciating the time you spend with your partner while also maintaining a level of independence.

Finally, if you are still having trouble with anger in your relationship after following the first seven steps, the eighth chapter talk about couples counseling. No one wants to resort to this step, but it sometimes becomes necessary when two personalities just can't seem to complement each other in the appropriate fashion.

Anger management can be difficult, if for no other reason than the simple fact that most people do not realize they need it. But for those who undergo the effort to manage their anger in a healthy fashion and work to foster a healthy relationship, the benefits cannot be overstated. Anyone who really cares about their relationship should take the following advice seriously. It can save a person from experiencing a nasty breakup, or even a divorce.

Chapter 1. Identify the Cause of Your Anger

This first step is rather intuitive, but that doesn't mean it doesn't need to be addressed. Many people think that the cause of their anger is simply their partner. Perhaps they believe the person they are with to have some sort of grating personality defect that needs to be changed if they are to enjoy being together. It should go without saying that this is an unhealthy way of thinking. If you assume that your partner is responsible for your angry mood swings, then you are probably not going to be together long. And if you continue to think that it is okay to blame others for your feelings, then you may as well stay single because you are not ready for the give and take that is required for the management of a healthy relationship.

Don't misunderstand the above paragraph. None of this is to say that your partner's actions or behaviors might not be related to your anger in one way or another, but rather that nobody can "make" you feel anything. If you are reacting angrily to something that your partner says or does, then you are going to have to recognize your part in this.

If you are the type of person that has a tendency to blame your partner for your anger, then you can start with a few basic steps in order to identify the root cause of your frustrations. First, try to hold up a mirror. In other words, identify what it is that your partner says or does that makes you angry, and try to figure out how those words or actions might resonate with you in other ways. For instance, say you lose your temper whenever your partner says something about your family or friends that upsets you. Is it possible that you subconsciously agree with what they are saying, and simply do not want to face the truth? Or maybe you disagree with what they are saying about your loved ones, but the qualities they are criticizing remind you of yourself. You might be amazed at how often this is the case.

Now, let's say you have tried holding up a mirror but you keep coming up blank. While the things that upset us in others are often things that upset us in ourselves, this is not always the case. Sometimes, they might simply remind us of other people. Maybe someone close to you has hurt you in the past, and certain behaviors that your partner exhibits have a way of reminding you about that person. This is sometimes the case with rather surprising behaviors. A man might get angry whenever he hears his wife or girlfriend singing while she does chores, because he had an abusive or neglectful mother who used to do the same thing. Maybe his mother wasn't abusive or neglectful, but simply dated men who had hurt him or even who had hurt her. All of these situations involving the man's potential experiences in his early life are significantly different from one another, yet they may all factor in when identifying the reason that his partner's singing makes him feel this inexplicable fury.

Now, the above example is somewhat unique. A person will often become angry at much more run-of-the-mill behaviors. A woman might be angry because her partner never cleans up after himself and lets her do all the work around the house. She might then yell at her husband or boyfriend because he never helps out. This might make him angry in return, because he feels that he works long hours and deserves more respect for this. In this type of occasion, both partners might identify the cause of their anger as the feeling that their lover does not fully appreciate them. Feeling appreciated is a basic human need, so it is not surprising by any means that some people are prone to emotional outbursts when they feel that this need has not been met by the person that they feel they should be able to trust the most.

The problem with situations like the one above is that they make it even easier to blame your anger on your partner. After all, didn't he or she get angry first? Weren't they the ones who flew off the handle without even stopping to consider your point of view?

If you find yourself asking questions like the ones above, then you have been brought full circle to the issue that was addressed at the beginning of this chapter, and it is now time to hold up that mirror. Yes, they yelled at you without considering your point of view. But when you retaliated, did you stop to consider theirs? Did you listen to what your partner was saying to you in the midst of their anger, or did you simply become indignant, assuming that you had been wronged and that your loved one's behavior had to be righted?

The point is that even though anger begets anger, that does not mean that you can lump all of the responsibility onto your partner for your own outbursts. "He/she did it first" is the exact line of reasoning that a child would take. Have a bit more self-respect than that, and approach the situation like an adult.

Identifying the true root causes of your anger can take a lot of courage. No one likes to admit that they are responsible for their own negative behaviors. It feels like admitting a weakness, but it is not. Admitting one's own faults is the first step to changing them, and it is a demonstration of true bravery and integrity. One you have learned to hold up a mirror and see that the reasons for the anger you feel toward your partner are actually more internal than external, you can begin to change things for the better.

Chapter 2. Learn How to Express Yourself

Whether your tempers tend to flare due to external or internal stimuli, there is one mistake that many people make that must be avoided at all costs. When many feel angry toward their partners, or even when they are using their partners to take out the anger they feel toward themselves, they often make the mistake of thinking that their loved ones should understand exactly how they are feeling and why they are feeling it.

You may love your significant other for a number of reasons, but the overwhelming odds are against the idea that any of those reasons pertain to his or her abilities as a mind reader. In other words, they will only know as much as you tell them. If you let your anger flow forth like a fountain and do not offer any sort of justifiable reason for it, then your partner will begin to think that you are simply unstable. If you allow them to hold onto this belief for too long, there is a good chance that they will leave you. Even worse, they may stay with you out of fear rather than out of love and understanding. This is not a healthy reason for maintaining a relationship.

Much like the idea of holding up a mirror as discussed in the previous chapter, learning how to express yourself can be a scary proposition. Rather than lashing out in anger whenever you are upset, you will be giving into your emotions and expressing your true vulnerability. Many may not realize it, but anger is essentially a defense mechanism that people use to try and look strong when they are feeling threatened. They may perceive something as a threat to their happiness, their way of life, or even just their desire for peace and quiet. As discussed in the last chapter, there is usually a reason that this sets them off and causes them to overreact.

Knowing what sets you off and why is useless, however, if you are not expressing these feelings to the best of your ability. There is a chance that when your relationship first began, you probably handled stress and anger quite well. At least, maybe you thought you did. You might have simply bottled things up and let them build until there was no way of suppressing your feelings any more. In your mind, your partner has caused you numerous upsets in the past, and you are justified in letting this out in whatever manner you see fit. In your partner's eyes, however, your outbursts and confusing and nonsensical because you have never reacted this way to their actions in the past.

This entire miscommunication could have been avoided if you had simply communicated your feelings when they first arose. There are several reasons that you might not have done this. Perhaps you thought that your mild annoyances would pass in due time and that there was no significant reason to address them. Maybe you were worried that anything which sounded like a criticism of your partner might hurt his or her feelings. But rest assured that letting your partner know your pet peeves would not hurt their feelings half as much as seeing you angry at them. Not by a long shot.

It is not only important to express how you feel, but to do so often. This may sound like clichéd advice, but try to stick to "I" statements rather than "you" statements. For instance, pretend that you recently flew off the handle because your lover spent a lot of money on a major purchase without consulting you, even though the two of you are currently struggling to stay above board in terms of rent and utilities. Do not approach the situation with a statement such as "*You* never consult me when spending money," or "We're struggling on rent because of *you*." Instead, try saying something to the effect of "*I* feel like my efforts to provide for us are underappreciated," or "*I* would really think that *we* should consult each other before making major purchases." This last statement also includes the word "we," showing that you consider yourself to be part of a team rather than one person who is engaged in conflict with another.

The point of expressing your feelings in this fashion is to allow your partner to understand how you feel, rather than simply placing blame. If they feel that they are becoming a scapegoat for your anger, they may become defensive. By stating your own feelings without making the issue all about them, you foster a sense of understanding between the two of you. They will respect this, and they will be more likely to hear you out. You may not get exactly what you want, but you will begin steps toward working out a compromise.

Bear in mind that communication is a two-way street. Your partner may have their own pet peeves that have been causing them anger or annoyance. When you express yourself to them, you might open up the floodgates for a great deal of communication regarding the ways in which the two of you have been causing each other frustration. Do not allow this to put you on the defensive. Hear them out. It may be uncomfortable at first, but this is a major step toward bettering your relationship. This step should not be overlooked by any means.

Of course, there are also times when it is just as important to refrain from expressing yourself. It is very important to know the difference between annoyances that must be addressed and things that you must simply let go if you do not want to hurt the one you love. The difference between healthy and unhealthy expression will be covered in the next chapter.

Chapter 3. Learn Not to Express Yourself

You might be reading the title of this chapter and wondering what it has to do with anger management. Your confusion can be easily forgiven, as this is not very intuitive. But keep in mind that the purpose of this book is to inform you specifically on how to manage your anger within a relationship. Based upon what you have read regarding the potential for one partner's emotions to affect the other's, part of managing your own sense of calm and well-being will be to do the same thing with your partner. This will help to mitigate the sources of friction between the two of you. One of the best ways to cut down on such frictions is also one of the easiest: you must simply know when to bite your tongue.

Sometimes, the fact that you feel as if you need to say something does not mean that your partner actually needs to hear it. When you express your feelings to your partner, you are not just expressing your vulnerabilities. You are not just telling him or her about your pet peeves, or about why certain behaviors have the propensity to bring out your angry side. These may be manners in which you are communicating on a deeper level, but you should never forget that on the surface you are still essentially telling your partner what it is you don't like about their behavior. Depending upon the sources of anger you've identified, you might even be criticizing their personality as a whole.

In the first chapter, you were presented with a hypothetical man who had deep emotional issues that were triggered when he was reminded of the way in which his mother used to sing to herself while performing housework. There were some variations on this hypothetical, one of which involved the mother suffering abuse while the man was left helplessly to watch, unable to help her in his youth. This must have been heart-wrenching for the man in question, but imagine how the mother would have felt if someone told her to stop singing, to stop bringing a little bit of light into her life when she was troubled.

If the hypothetical man of which we speak were to ask his wife or girlfriend why she sang when performing chores, he might be surprised to find that she has her own troubled history and that this act of song helps her to relieve the pain. He should no more want to deprive her of this relief than he would his own mother.

Now, you might be thinking that he doesn't need to command her to stop. After all, the last chapter presented you with the concept of using

"I" statements to address your loved one's behaviors without assigning blame. This is certainly the preferred method of expressing one's own feelings, but it is hardly full-proof. Just because your loved one is not as likely to become defensive does not mean they will not still feel some guilt for triggering your emotions.

With that in mind, you might apply this consideration to just about any of your partner's behaviors that trigger your anger. You were presented with another hypothetical in which your partner had made a substantial purchase when the two of you were struggling for money. But was this a selfish act? If they bought something frivolous, then perhaps it was. On the other hand, they may have purchased something that they thought would be good for the house. They may have even been trying to make you happy.

In short, there are times when you must hold off on expressing your feelings and wait until you actually understand the motivations behind your partner's actions.

Sometimes, the problem is not a need to understand your partner's motivations before expressing your feelings, but rather a need to bite your tongue entirely. If expressing the source of your frustrations is going to cause your partner any type of emotional harm, then your thoughts are better left unspoken. For instance, maybe your boyfriend, girlfriend or spouse is accompanying you to a work-related function and you had hoped that they would wear a particular outfit. The one they chose to wear instead is not one of your favorites, and this makes you angry.

Now take a step back from the above situation. Is it possible that they didn't wear the outfit you wanted them to wear because it doesn't fit them the same way as it once did? Would criticizing them for this, or even asking them questions about it, really do anything to help either one of you? Probably not. It's likely to make them feel bad about themselves, which might easily lead to a fight. The two of you may not fight immediately, but they may feel resentments toward you that fester over time until they become too much to bear.

Aside from the fact that this type of expression is unnecessary, it is also irrational. Even if the work function in question is important, it is not fair to get mad at your romantic partner on the basis of their appearance. As long as they put forth some effort and did not show up underdressed or sloppy, then there is no reason to feel as if they did not respect the importance of the event.

Situations like those above cannot be solved through shouting matches, because they do not need solutions to begin with. If you are able to really take a step back and see that your anger is sometimes irrational, then you will be able to figure out when you most need to bite your tongue. This will prevent you from saying something that may upset your partner, which in turn will prevent them from doing or saying something to intentionally upset you as an act of retaliation.

One final note on this: do not just bite your tongue because it may serve your anger management in the long run. If you really love the person with whom you are in a committed relationship, you will learn when to bite your tongue because it is the right thing to do.

Chapter 4. Set Some Healthy Boundaries

In the preceding chapters, you've been introduced to the need to express your feelings, as well as the need to let things go when this sort of expression is likely to hurt the one you love. Now, it's time to take a look at how to take the feelings you've expressed and turn them into healthy boundaries that your partner may respect.

Before going any further, please bear in mind that not all boundaries are healthy by any sense of the word. You are not trying to take control of another person's life. You are not trying to intimidate them into doing what you want, nor are you trying to set boundaries that will alienate you from your partner. If you find yourself trying to do these things, then you may want to question whether or not you should be in a relationship right now to begin with.

In other words, you should not even try to begin setting boundaries until you are completely confident that they are going to not only help you to manage your anger, but also to strengthen the relationship as a whole. If you are and your partner are not living together and they have made a mess of your bathroom sink or left clothes lying around your bedroom floor, then you may wish to set a boundary that they respect your living space and clean up after themselves. But you may not set insane boundaries such as restrictions against using the sink or anything else that might cause them to feel uncomfortable or unwelcome in your home. This will be quite damaging to the relationship, and you will likely find yourself with much more to be angry about in the future as a result.

The ability to set healthy boundaries is beneficial for a few reasons. First of all, it will help you to avoid the sources of anger that you have identified. As long as you are setting boundaries that are not overly strict or disrespectful of your love one's ability to express themselves as a person, then you will find your relationship operating on a much higher level of mutual respect.

The second major reason that setting boundaries can be a healthy tool for your anger management goes back to what was discussed in the first chapter about holding up a mirror, and how anger can be a defense mechanism against feelings of insecurity. By exhibiting the self-confidence (not to mention the confidence you must have in your partner in order to request such boundaries in the first place), you will ultimately find yourself feeling less vulnerable and more secure in yourself as a person. This inner strength will benefit you as a person and will make it easier to adopt a calmer and more peaceful attitude.

If you are having trouble believing that setting boundaries can help you to manage your anger, then think for a second about what will happen to you if you do not set healthy boundaries. Basically anything that makes you tick is likely to occur. Your personal space will be invaded by a partner who does not realize the value that you place on it. Your feelings will not be respected by someone who does not know what your feelings are to begin with. You will not only become resentful toward them, but you will become gradually more and more exhausted from trying to hide the way you feel.

Now, it should be said that you may sometimes wish to set boundaries that present something of a grey area. For instance, say there is something that you do not want to talk about. Perhaps something happened earlier in your life that was difficult for you, and your partner occasionally wishes to talk about it. It would appear that setting a boundary should be acceptable, as you are simply asking your partner to respect your feelings and your privacy.

In reality, however, it is much more complicated than that. You are not simply asking your partner to respect your feelings, you are asking your partner to allow you not to talk about them at all. And in asking your partner to respect your privacy to this degree, you are essentially telling them that they are not allowed to know who you are on the inside. It can be difficult to open up sometimes, even to the one you love the most. In some ways, it is harder than opening up to a stranger, because you know that you'll be seeing your partner again and that they'll be thinking about your secrets. But letting go of the things that you're holding onto on the inside will ultimately set you free, and your relationship will be enriched by the experience.

In short, never set unhealthy boundaries that make your partner become uncomfortable, and never set boundaries that prohibit your loved one from knowing who you really are. Either of these types of boundaries will become toxic, and your significant other may silently resent you for them. This might lead to fights later on down the road, at which point it will be harder to manage your anger.

Conversely, never try to please your significant other too much, either. By not setting boundaries, you will become the resentful one, and it may not be as long before anger management becomes a problem for you. If you really love your partner, and if you really love yourself, then you will prevent this from happening by setting healthy boundaries in advance. Ultimately, it will be better for both of you, and it will keep either of you from flying off the handle later on because you feel that your unspoken boundaries have not been respected by one another.

Chapter 5. Give Your Partner Equal Respect

This chapter should not surprise you, especially after what you have already read about the ways in which your partner's mood can affect yours. When you do something that upsets your partner, and they lash out at you in turn, it becomes all too easy to become defensive and to try and match their anger or even outdo them. Basically, when one partner becomes angry at the other, it has the potential to turn into a home run derby of sorts, with each partner topping the other until both are left feeling tired and defeated.

The way to prevent this from happening is to give your partner the same opportunities to set their own boundaries that were provided to you in the last chapter. Just like you, your significant other is a living, breathing person with their own pet peeves and things that make them feel as if their space has been invaded and their feelings not respected. It is integral that you prevent them from feeling this way by giving them the absolute respect that they deserve.

There are two basic ways in which you can give your partner this respect. The first is to begin respecting any boundaries they might already have in place. The second is to actually go out of your way to give them a chance to set any boundaries that they might have in mind.

The first is not always easy. If you'll remember, part of the problem with setting your own boundaries that was discussed in the previous chapter was the fact that you may sometimes already have boundaries set in place that you expect your significant other to respect despite having never actually stated them out loud.

Your partner may very well do the exact same thing. He or she will not always feel as if their boundaries should have to be stated. This goes back to the earlier chapters on expressing feelings in general. Sometimes, it is simply all too easy to feel as if our significant others should understand our wants and needs without having to actually say anything about them.

This means that you may sometimes have to try and read your significant other to figure out what their boundaries are. If they become angry at you for something, do not simply respond by getting angry back at them. This will turn into a larger fight that will potentially build over time. Instead, you should do your best to understand where they are coming from. Listen to what they are saying, and try to figure out whether or not you may have crossed an unspoken boundary of theirs. If you are able to identify any ways in which you may have done this, then do your best to keep this from happening in the future.

Of course, you do not have to simply wait for them to get angry at you for doing something wrong. You might try to show enough respect to keep them from getting angry at all. Think about what your own boundaries are, and make sure that you are not hypocritical in crossing any of those same boundaries with your loved one. If you know them really well, then you should have at least a semblance of an idea regarding the nature of their morals, values and ethics. This should make it much easier to respect their boundaries, even if they have not been formally set at any point in the past.

Now, suppose that you simply cannot figure out what your significant other's boundaries are. Perhaps you have found that they frequently become angry at you, even when you do not feel as if you could possibly have done anything wrong. Maybe you have even made absolutely certain that you never cross any of the same boundaries that you have set for yourself. Sometimes, your partner might just be difficult to read.

In these cases, you will need to go out of your way to make sure that your partner has made their boundaries known. This is similar to what was covered earlier about getting your partner to express their feelings, but in this case your specific goal is to ask what *you* can do differently to help them maintain their happiness in the relationship. This is more than simply asking them to express their feelings. This is asking them to set actual rules that you will agree to follow as a show of good faith, as well as a sign of your undying respect for the one you love.

Bear in mind that the boundaries set by your partner should follow the same rules as you were given for setting your own boundaries. You should not feel as if you have to follow any rules set by your significant other that might be considered unreasonable from an objective standpoint. If you feel as if respecting a certain boundary is going to make you feel resentful, and that it might actually make it harder for you to manage your anger in the relationship, then this is something that needs to be addressed early on. As the name of the chapter states, your task here is to show your partner *equal* respect, not to simply bow down to any demands they might choose to make.

The point of the last few chapters is that there must not only be a mutual sense of expression between two partners, but a mutual sense of respect as well. Each person in a relationship has the right to set their own boundaries with the assurance that, as long as their expectations are reasonable, they will be respected. It is as vital for you to respect your partner and the boundaries that they have set as it is for you to respect yourself and set your own boundaries. Simply ensure that each of you is setting boundaries that are healthy and reasonable, and the two of you are much less likely to become angry at one another for reasons that could have been easily avoided.

Chapter 6. Develop Hobbies As a Couple

Over the course of reading the preceding chapters, it should have become fairly evident to you that one of the primary sources of emotional disturbance in a relationship between two people is a lack of quality communication built upon a foundation of trust and mutual respect. One of the ways to help build these qualities between the two of you is to develop hobbies as a couple. This is also great for you as an individual, because you can find something you love to do that you are able to share with your partner.

Finding mutual hobbies to pursue with your significant other can be beneficial to the management of your anger in a number of ways. First of all, there is the fact that you are already going to be doing something that you potentially enjoy. You are also going to be sharing this hobby with someone you love, which is an additional benefit. In other words, you will be doing yourself a favor while cultivating a positive experience with the person you love the most. This will strengthen your relationship, and will hopefully keep you from needing to manage your anger in the first place by ensuring that you are able to maintain a positive mood.

There are a few different types of hobbies that you and your partner may enjoy, depending upon your particular tastes. Many common choices include exercise classes, which are great because they release endorphins and spur the body's creation of dopamine and serotonin. In other words, exercising helps to relieve stress and increase happiness. Doing this with your partner will help you to associate them with this feeling, which in turn should make it much easier to control your anger around them.

Other great hobbies to pursue with your partner include those which involve learning a new skill. For instance, you might consider taking a cooking class together. Not only will you be able to take the class together, but you will be able to take that skill home with you and continue cooking together in your own kitchen. If the two of you would rather skip the class altogether, you can still start cooking together in your own kitchen by buying meals with pre-packaged ingredients or by simply acquiring a decent cookbook and finding recipes that the two of you would like to make together from scratch.

Some couples may enjoy dance classes, which combine the two benefits described above. Not only do they provide exercise and all of the mood stabilizing benefits that come with it, but a new skill is learned that will allow couples to go out dancing. There are some couples who are more inclined to grow dissatisfied and angry with one another once the romance in their relationship begins to die down, and learning a skill that will allow the two of you to go on dates at new locations will help to counteract this unfortunate side effect of long-term relationships.

There are numerous other hobbies that couples may choose to pursue together. Some couples may enjoy less common types of outings, such as bird watching or even comic book conventions. All you need to do is find a shared interest with your partner and find a way to exploit this interest in order to begin doing things together. This will put both of you in a generally better mood, and your anger is less likely to get the better of you during daily interactions.

Since some of these hobbies involve learning new skills, there is a bit of a cautionary note that must be made. If you are a perfectionist, and if you sometimes find yourself losing your temper when your significant other makes a mistake, then you are going to need to learn how to control this instinct when pursuing a new hobby together.

Maybe you are the type of person who gets frustrated or angry when your partner steps on your toes during a dance class, for instance. You might be annoyed at the sheer discomfort of it, or you may even be angry that you feel embarrassed by having your partner make such a mistake in front of other people.

You should see this as an opportunity to work on your anger, learning to understand that your partner is a human who is prone to mess up occasionally. If the hobby you are pursuing together involves being in a public space where there are multiple other people present, then you might be a little bit less likely to lose your temper. In addition, you will hopefully come to see that your significant other is putting forth a lot of effort in order to do something with you that will strengthen your relationship and keep the two of you happy. This should be worth a lot of respect on your part.

Of course, you and your loved one do not technically have to take up an actual hobby in order to spend more time together and rekindle the romance and good feelings that were likely more present toward the beginning of your relationship. You might simply begin going on more dates while finding a way to keep things fresh. This might involve going to restaurants that you have not tried before, or simply going to see a movie every week and switching off who gets to pick the movie in question. It does not take much work to add just a little bit of spice to a relationship, although greater effort will generally yield greater rewards.

Whether you are pursuing a new hobby together or simply deciding to go on more dates as a couple, you will hopefully find yourself becoming more at ease as you spend more time with your partner. When learning a new skill together, you should learn to appreciate the fact that they are not perfect, but that they are a person with as many interests and passions as you. This should bring you closer together, making it easier for you to control your anger around you mate or spouse in the future.

Chapter 7. Develop Hobbies on Your Own

The previous chapter dealt largely with how spending more time with your significant other might put you in a better place and help you to appreciate them in a way that might mitigate any flare-ups in your temper. Now, it is time to discuss just the opposite. Sometimes, you need to be on your own, and you need to make sure that this time is spent in a worthwhile manner.

Developing your own hobbies will help you to maintain your calmness and sense of inner peace in a couple of different ways. First of all, it will help you to maintain your sense of independence. One potential cause of anger in a relationship is the feeling of being smothered. If you have ever found yourself feeling this way, then even the occasional bout of alone time might feel meaningless if you do not make the most of it. By finding new and exciting ways of enjoying your free time, you can feel as if being in a relationship has not stifled your ability to be your own person. This will lessen any unspoken resentments, conscious or subconscious, that you may feel toward your partner.

In addition to allowing you to feel as if you have maintained your independence, developing hobbies on your own will allow you to feel better as a person overall. For instance, one of the potential activities discussed in the previous chapter as a potential hobby to pursue with your loved one was exercise. If you are the self-conscious type, or if you simply do not enjoy exercising with your partner, then you may decide to pursue a more rigorous exercise routine on your own time. Again, this will help to stabilize your mood and will make it much easier to manage your anger on a day-to-day basis. The importance of stabilizing one's mood cannot be overstated when discussing the pursuit of anger management.

It is also important to have your own friends. Your romantic partner cannot constitute your entire social life. This will lead to frustration, which can explode into anger when it is built up enough over time. In other words, the important thing is not always necessarily to develop hobbies completely on your own, but simply to develop hobbies that are not primarily shared with your partner.

Similar to what was discussed in the last chapter, one does not always need to develop actual hobbies, but simply find a way of getting out of the house for something other than work or other obligations. If you are not satisfied with your life in general, then you are much more likely to take this out on your partner at some point or another. This is true even if you do not necessarily spend a great deal of time with one another. It is simply easier to blame one's romantic partner for their problems than to face the fact that the problem might be inaction on one's own part.

One of the most important things to remember, taking into account both this chapter and the one that precedes it, is to make every moment count. It cannot be said enough that the more one allows themselves to experience dissatisfaction, boredom, disappointment, loneliness, or any one of dozens of other negative emotions, the more likely they are to take it out on their significant other. It is not always that one actually blames the person they love for the feelings they experience, but simply that they are the easiest scapegoat for such emotions.

With that in mind, try to pick a hobby that meets your needs to the fullest extent possible. If you are interested in music, try taking lessons in playing an instrument or simply start going to concerts with your friends. If you are interested in sports, try to find some time to make it out to a few games or maybe even join a local recreational team. Whatever you choose to do, try to make sure that your activity of choice is in line with your biggest interests. This will make sure that you are happy with your choice.

If there is one word of caution that should be given in this chapter, it is that pursuing a new activity on your own or with friends may create a certain level of jealousy on the part of your romantic partner. Even if they happen to be understanding enough to understand your need to have your own life, that does not mean they will not sometimes wish that they could be a part of the activities that you are now enjoying by yourself or with others. This may cause a degree of tension between the two of you, which may result in arguments that cause your angry side to come out.

To counteract this, you should consider sharing your solo activity with your partner at least every once in a while. If you are going to concerts with friends, try inviting your loved one every so often. Even if they do not like the musicians you are going to see perform, they will likely still appreciate being invited. This will allow you to keep pursuing your own hobbies and interests without creating a rift between you and your romantic partner in the process.

Incorporating the advice given in this chapter and the advice given in the one before it can become a difficult balancing act. Most people have work as well as other various obligations they must attend to (such as family gatherings), leaving little free time left in the day. You are then charged with the task of figuring out how to divide this free time between time spent with your loved one and time spent with your friends or by yourself.

This can be difficult, but the payout is worth it. When you and your partner are not spending your free time together, you will both be free to pursue other activities independent of one another. This will result in more happiness for each of you in the long run, which will go a long way toward helping you to manage your anger when the going gets rough. The happier you are in general, the less likely you will be to give into outbursts when you become upset or frustrated.

Chapter 8. Consider Couples Counseling

Each of the above chapters concerns a method by which you may strengthen your relationship in order to reduce tension and help you to better manage your anger. Unfortunately, some people may try all of the above methods while finding that they still experience flares in their temper for reasons that they cannot seem to identify. If this is the case with you, then you are going to want to consider seeking the help of a professional who might be able to get to the root of the problem while examining more advanced ways of keeping your anger in check.

Couples counseling can be a useful tool for this. It is not quite the same as one-on-one therapy, because the counselor will not simply be looking at you and trying to assess the things in your past that might be responsible for your emotional reactions to various stimuli. Instead, the counselor will be looking at each person in the relationship and consulting them on how they might behave toward one another in order to bring out the best in each other.

Some people are afraid of couples counseling. They fear that seeking professional help is a sign that the relationship has failed, and that as soon as they consult a counselor they have essentially admitted that the relationship is beyond saving. This, however, is not really the case. Choosing to participate in couples counseling shows that you are dedicated to the one you love, and that you are willing to do anything it takes in order to save the relationship.

One of the most important things to remember when going through couples counseling is that you must take all suggestions that are given to you by your counselor. That does not mean that you should take most suggestions, except for a few suggestions concerning areas in which you think you still have some pretty good ideas. You must get over the notion that you know how to fix your relationship and manage your anger on your own, because if this were the case then you would not be in couples counseling to begin with.

For this reason, it bears repeating that you must take literally *every suggestion that is given to you by your counselor.* If something seems counterintuitive, or if something goes against the way in which you would normally handle a particular situation, then keep in mind that this might be a good thing. When someone who is licensed to handle situations such as yours has told you to do something, then you can generally count on them to know what they are talking about.

Many of the suggestions you receive in couples counseling may be somewhat commonplace. You might receive suggestions such as closing your eyes and counting to ten whenever you find yourself becoming more upset than you reasonably should be. You may receive a number of the same suggestions given to you by this book, especially in regard to strengthening your communication with your significant other and engaging yourself in activities that will reduce your general stress level. When receiving some of these suggestions, you will also hear some of the same principles that have been presented to you in the preceding chapters, such as the notion that one partner's tension can affect the other's mood, thereby creating an atmosphere of anger and dissatisfaction that pervades the relationship and makes things more difficult for all involved.

That said, the point of couples counseling is that you will also receive advice that is more tailored specifically to you and your partner. Your counselor may be able to suggest specific hobbies that the two of you might enjoy pursuing as a couple. Your counselor will also be able to provide you with insights regarding how you might strengthen your communication with one another. Counselors are generally good at reading people, so it should not take them too long to get a feel for the basic communication styles of each partner and make some recommendations that should greatly improve the relationship.

As you work through your relationship issues during your counseling sessions, you should find yourself becoming angry at your partner with much less frequency. Trust, love and understanding will come to replace doubt, annoyance and frustration. You and your significant other will have less to argue about, because you will learn to communicate on the same wavelength with one another. This is greatly important to fostering a healthy relationship in which each partner receives equal respect from the other.

Some people may be open to couples counseling, yet may still hesitate to set up a session because they are afraid of the cost. Professional therapy of any kind can sometimes be expensive, and couples counseling is generally no exception. However, you must ask yourself how much the relationship is worth to you. Odds are, you will not be able to express your answer in dollar signs. This means that, even if you may not have a great sum of wealth at the moment, signing up for at least one counseling session might be worth the money if you are able to experience any benefit to your relationship and to your ability to manage your anger. Talk it over with your romantic partner, and see if he or she agrees. If so, then you should schedule a session without delay. Even just one or two sessions will help you to start building the tools that you need to manage your anger in a manner that is healthy for both you and your partner.

Basically, the willingness to engage in couples counseling will take a bit of courage and open-mindedness. You will have to admit that your efforts up to this point have not helped you to manage your anger as well as you would like. If you can be honest enough with yourself to admit this, then you can benefit from the services of a professional who can hopefully teach you to become a calmer and more understanding lover.

The Worst-Case Scenario

Every chapter in this book up to this point has discussed potential reasons for your anger and ways in which you can try to manage your emotions for the betterment of your relationship. However, it is time to end by talking about what might happen if this cannot be done.

Before proceeding, it needs to be stated that finding yourself in the worst-case scenario is not a sign that you are a failure or that you will never be able to maintain a healthy relationship. It simply means that you were either not ready when you began this one, or that you were not with the right person. Either one of these things can be difficult to admit. Nobody wants to admit that they aren't ready to get what they want, nor do most people care to admit that the person they love is not necessarily the person that they are meant to be with.

If you find yourself in such a position, wherein you have tried following all of the above advice and simply cannot seem to manage your anger, then it may be time for a trial separation. In other words, you do not have to formally end the relationship right now, even if you are relatively certain that things are headed in that direction. Instead, you might consider simply taking some time apart. Use this time to get to know yourself a little better, and perhaps try some one-on-one therapy in order to work on your anger management in general before entering back into a relationship. If you do wind up getting back together, then you will both be glad that you took this time to work on yourself personally so that you can be a calmer, more stable, and much more dependable romantic partner.

On the off-chance that you do not end up getting back together, then you can still use everything that you have learned up to this point. The advice in this book, the lessons learned over the course of your relationship with your partner, and the things that you learned about yourself during your period of separation can all be considered to be building up to something better. Life is a long journey, and every leg of that journey helps you to grow as a person as long as you continue to process the lessons that have been laid before you and apply them to your future endeavors.

In fact, it might even be to your benefit if you do not wind up getting back together with your partner, as this will give you a chance to see just what can happen if you do not take your anger management seriously. You have seen the affects that your anger can have on a relationship, and you will therefore be much more likely to work at managing your anger in the future.

Of course, hopefully things will not get this bad. Keep in mind that this is simply the worst-case scenario. For some people, their romantic relationships may start to improve from the second they start applying the lessons provided in the very first chapter of this book. Others may start to experience positive changes about halfway through. Some may wind up following this book all the way to couples therapy, but will learn through their sessions how to manage their anger and strengthen their relationship before they wind up being separated, broken up, or divorced.

Even if you are one of the lucky few who started to experience positive changes early in the reading, do not let that deter you from continuing to follow the advice in this book once your relationship has improved. If you were prone to outbursts of anger in the past, then you just might find yourself experiencing these outbursts again in the future if you do not continue to work on yourself and your relationship.

If you do find yourself experiencing such outbursts again, do not fret. You already know what to do. Start by trying to identify the root cause of your frustrations, and follow this up by expressing yourself to your partner. Of course, remember that there are situations in which you should not express yourself, but rather simply learn to let things go. If the problem is that you feel a boundary has not been respected, then make sure you are able to relate this to your partner in a healthy way. If the problem is that there are simply tensions between you that may be coming from your partner's end, then give him or her a chance to express themselves and tell you whether or not you have been crossing any of their boundaries by mistake. Also do not forget to continue pursuing new life-enriching activities, both on your own and as a couple. And if none of these things seem to help, then you might try returning to couples counseling for a few more sessions in order to help the two of you iron things out.

You may occasionally have to go through this routine again, but there is no shame in that. The sheer fact that you are willing to do so is a sign that you have come a long way. You are no longer a person who gives into their anger and lashes out emotionally at the ones they love, but rather a person who appreciates the gift of romance enough to better themselves in order to keep pursuing it. As long as your heart is in the right place, and as long as you are willing to keep working on yourself, then there just may be hope for your romantic future no matter how things have been in the past.

Just stay calm, and stay positive.

www.ingramcontent.com/pod-product-compliance
Lightning Source LLC
Chambersburg PA
CBHW052201110526
44591CB00012B/2034